THE BOOK OF EXTRA

"Motivational Insights to Help Realize Your EXTRA Ordinary Potential"

CELESTE CUFFIE

The Book of Extra

No Ill Intent

This book is designed to provided inspiration and motivation to our readers through the author's experiences. It is sold with the understanding with the publisher is not engaged to render any psychological, legal, or any other kind of professional advice. The content is the sole expression and opinion of its author and not necessarily that of the publisher. Neither the publisher nor the author shall have liability nor responsibility to any person or entity with respect to any loss or damage caused, or alleged to have been caused directly or indirectly by the information contained in this book.

THE BOOK OF EXTRA

"MOTIVATIONAL INSIGHTS TO HELP REALIZE YOUR EXTRA ORDINARY POTENTIAL"

CELESTE CUFFIE

www.celestecuffie.com Twitter-@Celesteempowers

ISBN-13: 978-0692711026
(Life Empowered Consulting Services)

ISBN-10: 0692711023

All rights reserved. No parts of this publication may be reproduced, stored in any retrieval system, or transmitted in any forms or by any means, electronic, mechanical, recording, or otherwise, without the prior permission of Celeste Cuffie. US, ©copyright 2016 Celeste Cuffie Manufactured in the United States.

DEDICATION

I want to take a moment to say thank you to all of the great people that I have been able to connect with. I dedicate this book to you.

To you, my family and friends, who have loved, supported, and encouraged me throughout my journey. I have been blessed to truly have a village to support me. Not only as a child but as an adult.

There are not enough words to say about all of those who have chosen to endure with me through the opportunities and obstacles of life, but I do want to say Thank you. From my heart, thank you.

Thank you to all that have taken the time out to not only invest in me, but to also invest in yourself. I am confident that there is something that is in this "Book of Extra" that will give you that "extra" that you need to go further, try harder, and endure longer, until ultimately, you accomplish your goal. That is what it is about. You can do it!!! I am merely your cheerleader.

I honor those that are no longer with me who cannot hear my "thank you" but were intricate parts of my life. With all that I have, I will do my best to make them proud by pouring into others, just as they poured into me.

In Memory Of:

Tom Stevens
Rose Stevens
Jonathan Cuffie
Florida Sheppard
Tina Cowan Wynn

TABLE OF CONTENTS

Intro 1

Note To Self 16

Nothing Beats A Failure But A Try 23

Everyone Is An Example 24

You Are Free 25

We Need And Value Structure 27

We Need The Sun And Rain........................... 28

The Power Of One 29

Follow God's Path For You 30

Starting Today 31

How To Have A Productive Day..................... 32

Greatness Is There.. 33

Expand Your Connections.............................. 34

Obstacles = Opportunities............................. 35

Your Mind Determines The Matter 36

Seeing The Beauty In Turmoil........................ 37

Sometimes, You Must Walk Alone 38

You Were Meant To Be Here......................... 39

Stretching During Downtime......................... 40

Your Vision Is Yours, Don't Give It Away 41

Understand Your Qualities 42

You Have To Want To 43

Three Lessons Today 44

Learn And Grow On 46

Support Helps 47

Some Things May Not Be In Balance 49

Pour Out Of Yourself, It Wasn't About You 50

Things To Remember For A Great Life 52

Better Or Worse 54

What Label Matters 56

Four Keys To Assessing Your Past 57

Pour Into Others Only What They Can Handle 58

Mirror The Greatness 59

Ten Keys To Great Relationships 61

Get Up 62

Grateful For Resources 63

Career Choices 64

Eight Steps To A Great Day! 66

How To Realize And Exceed Your Goals 67

How To Find The Greatness In People 68

Five Keys To Staying Encouraged 69

Live On Purpose 71

Six Keys To Handling Challenging Situations 72

Cultivate You 74

Two Times 75

Just Get There! 76

Stay Challenged 77

Appearances 78

The Resilience In Weeds 79

Determination Can Spark Creativity 80

Work At It! 81

Stay Connected 82

Move Beyond Your Emotions 83

Never Too Late 84

Opportunities 85

Slow Down, But Don't Stop 86

Time, Resources, And Money 87

Be The Best You 88

Conclusion Of The Matter 89

My Final Thoughts To You!! 91

FOREWORD

I've heard it said that the difference between ordinary and extraordinary people is literally one word…"extra". In life, when we look at the people we admire, we tend to believe they have extra "ingredients" within them that others don't. This "magic" of sorts, seems to have propelled them towards reaching a pinnacle accomplishment. What if some of the magic isn't propelled by innate ingredients at all?

No one would argue that extra preparation, determination, or persistence of an individual can make the difference be- tween coming in first or second whether it be running a race, competing for a job, or more simply, interacting with the people we care about.

The "Book of Extra" highlights how life experiences that we take for granted as routine, can be powerful teaching moments. Many people endure a seemingly never-ending list of tasks as part of being parents, spouses, employees, and just orchestrating the day-to-day details of life. Sometimes how people perceive a particular task, event, or person is normally based on historical reference, past experience, and/or learned behaviors. Similar to adjusting the focus on a projector, what if we could refine our view of these moments in life to achieve extraordinary clarity and capability?

What if…we could see traffic and construction on grueling commutes as a metaphor for patience, persistence, and determination?

What if…we could invest an hour a week to stretch ourselves not just physically, but in terms of capability by trying something new?

What if…we could recognize and embrace trials and obstacles as teachable moments that help us iterate towards our desired outcome?

These "what if's" are just extra things we can do to complement things we're already doing. The next time you enjoy a salad, entrée, or dessert think about what you did to complement that meal and why? The Book of Extra is kind of like that extra seasoning or sauce. Just a little smidge of this or a little bit extra of that can go a long way to enhancing your experience in life.

I hope you enjoy this book as I did and use it as motivation to activate and apply the "extra" already within you to live a more fulfilled life.

- Sheldon I Cuffie

PROLOGUE

In 2012, God shared with me that I had the ability to do all things concerning my career, my education, and my family. I needed to begin to focus on what He purposed for me. He challenged me to be attentive to life and the lessons that could be drawn from my daily activities. I took His challenge. I was also challenged to archive and share them. Soon after, I started my business, Life Empowered Consulting Services. I was exposed to even more lessons and teachable moments. Capturing those moments is how the "Book of Extra" began. I want to share those lessons with you.

Intro

Growing up as a child, there were so many things I was sheltered from. Certainly, I did have the typical things such as falling off a bike, having fights at school, and getting bad grades, but overall, I truly was sheltered. It wasn't until I was an adult that I began to see and experience true trials and hardships. Now, granted, at 12 years old, no one could have told me that I would love again after my first love broke my heart. (It's funny even saying that.) Nonetheless, what I experienced as a child was nothing compared to the challenges of today.

I am sure this is why I encourage my children to embrace being a child. My children have the ability that all children should have but do not - to rest in the arms and safety of Mom and Dad. It is unfortunate, the reality of some of our children (and adults for that matter) who have yet to find safety and security in, at the very minimum, themselves. I am not sure what has happened. Where did our confidence in ourselves go? Where did our confidence in each other go?

According to the World Giving Map 2013, the United States has ranked number 1 for being the most benevolent country in the world, yet we feel as though we can't trust each other. People literally leave the country to adopt children to provide them with good homes and love, yet there are children wandering around streets every day looking for food and a warm place. I know that the Deuteronomy 15: 7 says there always will be poor among us, but this seems like a different kind of poor; we know they need, and we would rather throw out the food than share it with someone else. So not only have we become poor with our giving, but also with our compassion.

I think what makes matters worse is that as a result of the bubble of protection that many of us have grown up in, we make the assumption that others have had the same opportunity. This simply isn't accurate. Everyone in life has NOT been afforded the same opportunity. However, I do believe that everyone has opportunity. There are many instances where individuals may have had everything needed to be successful and to capitalize on their opportunities, but they just didn't. Conversely, we are also of those who statistically are destined for failure, but have managed to seize every possible opportunity and have become great successes as a result. But again, the commonality in both is simply opportunity.

What tends to be even more disheartening about that situation is sometimes, from those that didn't seize their opportunity, they seem to convey a since of entitlement. For example, if "Nancy" the nurse is perceived as successful, then "Helen" the homeless woman approaches Nancy as if she is obligated to provide her with some assistance. I am not sure where the line lies, but what I am sure of is that these are the types of situations that create hesitation in helping.
I share this because as individuals, in whatever state that we are in, we have to be mindful of each other and help be creators of opportunity. Nancy should help Helen, but also point her to where she can get out of her

situation. Helen, should be appreciative knowing that Nancy doesn't owe her, but she helps from the kindness of her heart. Helen's appreciation and gratefulness keeps Nancy's heart open to help others.

During my personal life's journey, I have learned many things about myself. Additionally, I have also begun to embrace those things. It is the successes of life and the failures of life that have taught me the wisdom that I am going to share with you. I am excited about the opportunity to share these life's lessons as the people in my life have shared them with me.

It is so interesting to really go through the process of learning who you are. While I say that, I say it with the caveat of understanding that as we journey through life, we evolve. Yes, we do. Who we are today is not the same as who we were yesterday, and who we are today, very likely will not be who we are going in the future. However, the truth is that we are still the same person. However, as we proceed on the daily activities of life, who we "thought" we were sheds, and the true, real us begins to show.

I remember some time ago taking a personality profile assessment. This assessment was quite interesting because it revealed two things about me. The first was who I thought I should be, and the second was who I really was. This is something that I am sure we battle with every day. Who are we, and who do we think we should be?

Funny story... My husband and I were talking about

having a celebration at our home. He began to talk about the wear and tear on the house because of all of our "festivities." I then went on to say, "But that's why we have the house, so that we can entertain. That's who I am!" He gave me a look, so I followed up with a small tap dance and a "ta-da." He began laughing hysterically and just shook his head.

"Finally," I said to myself. It took me nearly 40 years to embrace who I am and to like it. This feels good. It feels good to know that I love people, and I love socializing, and I love sharing, and I love helping, and I love cheering. Yes. This is who I am.

What's more interesting is that it feels completely weird to have it reciprocated. I have connected with so many great people, and when they show me love, I often tear up. It's amazing to me that I have been so focused on giving that I didn't really ask to receive it, so I didn't expect it. But when I receive it, wow, does it feel good.

"How did I get to this point?" you ask... Good question. There were a series of resources that I used. I want to share them in a list format so that you can clearly identify and take advantage of them.
- Myers-Briggs assessment
- Strengths finder assessment
- Slowing down in life enough to pay attention to the moments in my life in which I was the happiest
- Making a mental note of those moments and working to recreate those moments on a daily basis
- Honesty with myself

I suppose that in life, we can lie to anyone we want to, but the one person I suggest that we don't lie to is ourselves. Meaning, that if you don't drink, then don't drink. If you don't smoke, don't smoke. That doesn't take away from what anyone else does, but it only speaks to what you do. When you make those choices, don't feel bad; fitting in isn't all it's cracked up to be anyway. If you are so busy trying to fit in, who's going to lead out? And yes, I get it... leading isn't all it's cracked up to be either, but if it has to be done, and it does, who better to do it than you? We often get nervous about the word "leading," but I have learned that leading is merely serving. That's whether you are serving your family, your friends, your colleagues, or your religious organization. It's all leading and serving. I would really say that the main difference between leading and serving is the spirit behind it and the proactivity of doing it.

When I discuss you being who you are and embracing it, I am referring to the pure and kind hearted you, not from a heart of animosity, anger and bitterness. Believe it or not, even though there are some things that can really get under your skin, you have the power to not allow it to change you for the worse. Truthfully, many of the behaviors that we portray are symptoms of a root cause. That's why understanding yourself is so important. This is called emotional intelligence, understanding your emotions and what triggers them.

Through my dear friend Nicole, I learned that according to 20th century psychologist and theorist Robert Plutchik, there are eight primary emotions:

- Trust
- Joy
- Anticipation
- Anger
- Disgust
- Sadness
- Surprise
- Fear

Plutchik goes on to suggest that, "All other emotions are mixed or derivative states; that is, they occur as combinations, mixtures, or compounds of the (8) primary emotions." Below are just some examples:

A combination of
- Joy & Trust = Love
- Anticipation & Fear = Anxiety
- Surprise & Sadness = Disappointment
- Anger & Disgust = Contempt

This is definitely an interesting theory that may not be believed by all, but I must say during my many, many years of leading teams - and I have listened to much of the chaos that can ensue as a result of misunderstanding - I have to believe there is quite a bit of merit to this theory. During those dialogs that I referred to, as I listened to what the person was saying and not saying, I often found the behavior was a symptom of one of the root causes indicated (usually fear). It's important that you assess yourself to make that determination. After you figure those items out, you then learn and apply how to mitigate them.

Hopefully, if someone has backstabbing tendencies, it's not because they are a backstabber by nature. Rather, due to a root emotion, such as fear, and years of behaving in this manner, you just haven't learned a better way yet. Rest assured, being a backstabber is not a good thing even if you know why you do it, and there is a better way. I believe that we were born in sin and shaped in inequity just as the Bible says in Psalms 51:5, but I don't believe that we have to stay there.

Now, if you never find out why you do certain things, but you know that they are hurtful, deceitful, and malicious, then you are still challenged to stop those behaviors. While it is important to me to understand why things happen, when it's all said and done, if there is a change that is needed, it is up to us to make that change regardless of why.

I am learning to be aware of me. This awareness of yourself can be the difference in life, taking the time to learn you and appreciate you. As a leader and a servant, in order to really thrive, you have to identify things that will make you happy. As you ponder that, think about the stuff that you have. Take a moment to write a list of the stuff that you have that makes you happy, such as shoes. Then on the other side, list the intangible things that you have that also make you happy, such as quiet.

When looking at both lists, ask yourself what things would you be okay without and what you want to make sure you have for a very long time. My short list of stuff is my physical home and my job. My short list of intangibles are time, family, opportunity, passion, peace, and motivation. And when I look at it time and time again, what I want, need, and don't want to give up are those intangible items. So my priority is keeping the balance of both.

I am also learning to accept guidance and support from others. While understanding that life is filled with good and not-so-good people, I think it's important that we learn from others.

Think of the worst person in the world to you. Describe from your perspective why he/she is the worst, and then learn what NOT to do from that individual. Also, do the opposite from the person who you think is wonderful. Learn what to do and do it. Learning skills and characteristics from either person would also be growth for you. Still being you, you have the ability to adapt the skills and characteristics that will help shape you.

Communication is another big one. I have learned not only how to communicate with myself but with others as well. It's not enough to speak greatness into the lives of others, but I should also be able to confidently speak greatness into my life with the perseverance to execute what I have spoken and mapped out.

Lastly, but certainly not least, is your understanding of the word of God. Allow that to be the tool that will further mold you into the person that God has created.

So there it is, those are things that I did to learn me, and feel free to leverage any of those to help you learn you as well. One more thing I would add is this... One of the main things that I believe in doing is helping others. That's a primary reason for writing this second book, to share the lessons I have learned. As you learn you, I encourage you to help others as well.

As you read through this book, you may see conflicting ideas, but that's because I have learned that my perspective is not the only perspective. As you are putting together the strategies to make the best of your life, you have to see both sides and balance the bitter with the sweet, or, in this example, your perspective today with other perspectives tomorrow.

Each of these lessons were birthed from different places in my life. They could have been good days, not-so-good days, great, or horrible days for that matter. But either way, they came forth. The question that remains is how do we place perspective around those moments, issues, challenges, and opportunities in life? How do we place a framework around them in such a way that each moment that we experience is designed to get us closer to our destination?

I want to take a few moments to answer that question. For me, it is very simple. 1) My faith in God, 2) knowing my purpose has not been fulfilled, and 3) gathering the experiences, finding the lessons, and bundling them all together to create great results.

As a Believer, I have to know that God is in control. While it seems like chaos to me, and my life seems to be spinning uncontrollably, my constant is HIM. This awareness of who is in control is paramount when dealing with both the good and the bad times.

According to a survey done at the University of Illinois, using Twitter as its source of data, Christians are happier. This survey taken in 2013, http://religion.blogs.cnn.com/2013/06/28/christians- happier-than-atheists-at-least-on-twitter/, proved the fact that believers, not just Christians, are healthier, happier people. It is important that I acknowledge and stay committed to Him in the good and the bad times because of the benefits. It's much like riding a bike. If you are able to ride it when the sun is out, then the process to ride is the same when there is no sun.

We have to form the habit to love Him, serve Him, and trust Him when things are good so that when difficulties arise, habits have already been formed, and you naturally do what you know to do. This is why firemen practice the job of firefighting when there is no actual fire, and police officers practice the job of crime fighting when there is no actual crime, so that when it's time to actually do it, it is second nature. Now, of course, that first couple of times may make you hesitant, but after a while, all of your training kicks in, and I am confident that you will know exactly what to do. But are you confident in that?

I had a friend tell me all of these great things that she desires to accomplish. However, she has not begun the process. Her reason for that was failure. She didn't want to fail. I certainly respect the fear; however, if the fear of failure is the reason for not trying, then one is successful at failure. I talked about, in my first book, the need to fear failure AND success if we are going to fear. My main premise is still the same: you have to try. Failure is a matter of perspective. Actually, I even see failure as a success. Think of doing a hypothesis. In understanding a hypothesis, you have to go through a series of tests that may or may not validate your educated guess. These tests will either substantiate or disprove your thought or idea. As a result of this testing, you figure out what works and what doesn't. The only way you do that is through the testing. Just because the test doesn't net the desired result doesn't mean it failed, it just means that you are successful at finding out what didn't work. See... it's all in the perspective.

What do you see when you see obstacles? From where, does your frame of reference come? Is it optimistic or pessimistic? Now, we have just talked about being real with yourself, so let's do a little test. This should tell you what provide some insight, just in case you aren't quite sure.

Optimism

To measure your optimism level with this test, indicate your response to each item below:

A--strongly agree; B--agree; C--feel neutral; D--disagree; E—strongly disagree.

Note: Don't let your answer to one question influence another.

1. In uncertain times, I usually expect the best.
2. It's easy for me to relax.
3. If something can go wrong for me, it will.
4. I'm always optimistic about my future.
5. I enjoy my friends a lot.
6. It's important for me to keep busy.
7. I hardly ever expect things to go my way.
8. I don't get upset too easily.
9. I rarely count on good things happening to me.
10. Overall, I expect more good things to happen to me than bad.

How to calculate the results:

Cross out or ignore your answers to items 2, 5, 6, and 8. Those are fillers.

Subtotal your scores for items 1, 4, and 10 as follows: A is 4 points; B--3; C--2; D--1; E-- 0.

Subtotal your scores for items 3, 7, and 9 as follows: A is 0 points; B--1; C--2; D--3; E-- 4.

Add those subtotals for an overall optimism score.

The range is from 0 to 24, from extreme pessimism to

extreme optimism, with virtual neutrality being the midpoint, 12.   Source: American Psychological Assn., 1994.

Now that you know your optimism or pessimism level, what do you do with it? Well, that's easy. Look at where you are, and decide where you want to be. Here are three phases (7 days each) that you can do. If you want to become optimistic, do phases 1-3. If you want to increase your optimism, do phases 2-3, and if you just need to maintain your optimism, do phase 3.

If you want to increase your optimism, begin with Phase One.

Phase One

Think back to yesterday, and identify something that happened negatively.
- Look for the positive lesson in it.
- Reflect on what you learned from that situation.
- Apply what you have learned.
- Tell God thank you for the lesson.

Repeat this for 7 days.

Phase Two

On day eight, do the following:
- At the end of the day, identify something that happened positively.

- Celebrate the positive in it.
- Reflect on what you learned from that situation.
- Apply what you have learned.
- Tell God thank you for the lesson.

Repeat this for 7 days.

Phase Three

On day 15, do the following:

As you go through your day, look at every situation (positive or negative) as an opportunity to learn something.

- Celebrate your ability to learn and grow from life's lessons.
- Smile as you are learning and embracing your growth.
- Share what you have learned with others.
- Tell God thank you for the lesson.

Repeat this for 7 days.

At this point, you have accomplished four items. 1) You have changed your perspective, 2) you have grown through life's lessons, 3) you have helped someone else, and 4) you have celebrated in your journey.

Throughout this book, you will find motivational thoughts, activities, and stories that are geared towards helping you be the very best you that you can be, empowering you to tap into your "extra". While I can certainly encourage, motivate, and support you, it is up to you make it happen.

I am confident that, if you have this book, then you can certainly do it. This is the first step to getting to where you want to be.

Every thought, goal, dream, and aspiration, will begin in your mind and end with your activities, your perseverance, and your commitment.

In my first book, "Looking Back, then Moving Forward," I share with you some very intimate things about my journey thus far. In this book, I really want you to walk away with the mind, passion, and tools to continue your journey with joy, peace, and endurance.

This book is broken into two main sections, "Note to Self" and "Extraordinary Insights." The "Note to Self" is 90 statements, affirmations, and reminders. Take one at a time, read them, internalize them, and keep them in your spirit throughout the day. Apply what the affirmation is to your life. Extraordinary Insights are short stories, lessons and tips, that will help you to tap into your extraordinary potential.

NOTE TO SELF

In this section, you will find various statements that you can take and meditate on as friendly reminders to keep you encouraged and focused on your priorities.

1. There is greatness in you. However, please don't make others look so hard to see it. Just let it show.
2. Enjoy being you!
3. As leader, choose to follow change-makers. Who are you following?
4. Trouble can do one of two things: make you or break you. You get to make that choice.
5. Appreciate the journey, looking forward to the destination.
6. When you feel you are not good enough, just know that you are!
7. Live life empowered!
8. You are the best you walking the earth today!
9. Learn something about myself every day. Wow You.
10. Celebrating the greatness of others also acknowledges of the greatness of you.
11. You simply have to believe.

12. Greatness is in the atmosphere. If you don't feel it, then check where you are.

13. Be excited about the new day coming.

14. Even in loss, there should be a celebration of the gain, such as time, encouragement, support, etc.

15. If you are the greatest thing in your circle, then you need a new circle.

16. When your attitude is right, even grey clouds and traffic jams are beautiful.

17. Start to really appreciate the journey, as it helps define the value of the destination.

18. Do yourself a favor. Forgive someone else.

19. You have to deal with it so that you can heal from it.

20. It's a great day with great things! Embrace it!

21. Recognize your own qualities.

22. Embrace your own vision.

23. Being you is so refreshing and easy.

24. Today is a gift for you to be a blessing to others. You are a conduit transferring the gift from God to others.

25. Being better is your goal. How are you doing at it?

26. In order to find your purpose, you have to experience the search.

27. Greatness is active 24/7.

28. Don't give your vision away.

29. What you need is inside of you.

30. You are capable to do more than you even know.

31. When you want a larger territory, you have to prepare to walk the span of it.

32. Greatness follows greatness.

33. Learning life's lessons may be difficult, but it will also be unforgettable.

34. Be grateful that pain does have a purpose.

35. Sometimes you have to just stop and enjoy where you are, even if it's not where you want to be.

36. Grow on, and keep on moving.

37. Be open and inspired to be better by the young and the old.

38. Pursue your purpose with passion and perseverance. No one else can do that for you.

39. Being present is being attentive and aware - not just being there.

40. Sometimes, walking alone is the only way to walk. It helps you to truly identify your hindrances because it's only you.

41. Better comes at a cost. You may have to sacrifice, but it's worth it.

42. Accountability is real, no matter who you are.

43. Take advantage of your gift, and share it with others.

44. Be responsible and accountable for you.

45. Select a day to reflect on the week and celebrate making it through.

46. Hope! If you have it, then you have something! If you don't, get some!

47. True beauty radiates… it can be blinding

48. Sometimes, others will surprise you - pleasantly.

49. Each day is a gift. Treasure it!

50. Take one step at a time and move forward.

51. Opportunity: don't let it pass you by.

52. Don't be afraid to live.

53. In order to live an empowered life, you must live.

54. Step out. You might be fearful, but you won't be sorry.

55. Strategy for life: live it to the fullest.

56. Plan, implement, and maintain for greatness.

57. Declare your life is good.

58. We have to believe in God.

59. Don't be afraid to be you.

60. It feels good to walk into your future. You have something to live for.

61. There's a silver lining in every cloud.

62. Build and grow forward.

63. Sometimes we have to go back to the core of who we are and build from there.

64. When you know it's over, you have to let it go and continue to move forward.

65. Sometimes, we have to just allow it to be what it is.

66. When everyone is looking down, keep your head up.

67. Where you are today isn't where you will always be. Don't allow what you say and do today to bring embarrassment tomorrow.

68. Navigate your challenges with grace.

69. Walking into your purpose also means walking out of things that were not.

70. While you may be nervous about branching out, be terrified about staying in this box and not realizing your destiny.

71. Be positive or be quiet.

72. Think of yourself as a person with loved ones, emotions, fears, hopes, and dreams. Think of others in the same way. Now treat them as such.

73. You are not the same. You are better.

74. You need courage to succeed and fail.

75. There is hope. As long as there is life, there is hope.

76. There's nothing wrong with loving.

77. Make educated decisions, not emotional ones.

78. We must allow our actions to line up with His word.

79. Leadership requires leaders and followers.

80. Opportunity is in the air - breathe it in.

81. Accepting average is not okay.

82. When your circle isn't large enough, open it up.

83. It always starts with one.

84. No one can beat you being you.

85. You control you.

86. When you push others to be better, you become better yourself.

87. Give thanks on purpose.

88. Although old habits die hard, but they still die.

89. Success is not emotional, it's success.

90. Keep God first - study and understand His word. Life's lessons are in there.

Nothing Beats A Failure But A Try

Regardless of a failure, if you keep trying, you can succeed. Understand that if you try and fail, you have learned what not to do, so whatever your efforts are in, they are progressive. However, if you don't try, failure is certain, and while others will learn what not to do through you, I have to believe that guaranteed failure was not your goal.

During Your Journey... Implement patience, perseverance, and proactivity while striving to your goals. If you do, you are sure to achieve them

EVERYONE IS AN EXAMPLE

We all are going to meet a large variety people in our lifetimes, and in their own way, they can and will teach us something. During those interactions, characteristics or behaviors that we either love or not, will be identified. From there, a decision to emulate or not emulate those behaviors should be made. Before the implementation of the decision is made, consider the consequences of the behaviors.

For example, if you encounter someone who speaks and behaves in an uplifting manner, ask yourself if this is a characteristic you would like to embody. If the answer is yes, then consider the consequences of this new behavior. In this example, the consequences would be positive goals being met and living in an empowered atmosphere. From there, you simply apply this new methodology to your life.

During Your Journey... Become a life learner. Learn from everyone you come into contact with.

You Are Free

Many years ago, I had a cat named "Kitty." I got her when she was six weeks old. She was a beautiful black and white mixed breed. At the time, my husband, Kitty, and I lived in a four-story apartment building. As Kitty got older, she began to get curious about what was outside the apartment. So when I would open the door to the hallway, initially she began to peek out. Soon after, she would cautiously walk out into the long hallway.

Then I found myself apprehensive to open the door because I knew that Kitty was going to now dash into the hall, and I would have to chase her up and down the hall to get her back into the apartment. Then one day, something happened. I opened the door, and I saw her running. I immediately pushed the door, trying to close it before she got out. In that attempt, she was accidentally hit by the door, and it really startled her. From that point on, she never tried to go out the door again. I left it open for extended periods of time, but she wouldn't even bother going near it. That one event caused her to never try again.

Often, we have an experience that we allow to change our very lives. It puts us in a bondage that keeps us from even trying to move forward. We resolve that we are destined to be failures, mediocre, or stagnant.

However, that's not true. We are not in captivity. We are not restricted from success. Granted, it's not easy, but it's not impossible. The door is open for you to walk into your future. You are equipped to operate freely with the power, brilliance, and creativity that dwells inside of you. So do it!

During Your Journey... See your destiny and make a plan to achieve it. Write it down, and then take the steps that you documented to accomplish your goals.

WE NEED AND VALUE STRUCTURE

The term freedom, I must admit, is used rather loosely. We want the freedom to make decisions, freedom to go where we want, and freedom to live how we choose. However, it is interesting how we want that, but what we need are guidelines to help us live those free lives. Watching the news and seeing all of the terrible things that people are doing to each other in this world with "structure," it is very difficult to imagine living in a world without it. Although things do not always occur in the manner in which I may prefer them to, I must say that I am at least appreciative of the structure that is in place. If the structure isn't meeting the ultimate need, then work to mold it into what it should be.

During Your Journey... Look at your homes and communities, appreciate that there is some semblance of structure. Identify areas of improvement if applicable, and work to make the improvements.

WE NEED THE SUN AND RAIN

I was thinking about the weather today. Some days are really hot, and others are just perfect with a subtle breeze moving through the trees. However, in the warmth of consistent sun, I have also begun to notice that the plants are dying, the lakes are receding, and the crops are not growing. But sunny, hot weather is what some of us dream of, especially during the heart of the winter - warmth and sun.

This brought me to the realization that no matter how much sun we want, we NEED the rain. So to say it differently, no matter how many good days we have, we MUST have some bad ones. The bad days really create the groundwork for appreciating the good days and not taking them for granted. In addition, it brings balance. The flowers are a result of the sun and the rain - not either one independently.

During Your Journey... Think of something negative that occurred in your life, and then take a moment to be grateful that it's no longer there! Celebrate the peaks and valleys of life!

THE POWER OF ONE

There are so many instances in life when we feel as though we want to do something, but we feel helpless. We are often guilty of feeling as though, "If we can't help everyone, why bother helping anyone?" From that thought, we then begin to fear starting something and not completing it, so we hesitate, or even worse, we simply do not start it at all.

Depending on what we are striving to do, we have to recognize that there are many situations in which doing something, regardless of how large or small it is, is better than doing nothing at all. In addition to that, we don't need a large committee, we don't need formal approval; we just need the passion, the drive, and the willingness to step out and do something. As a result, you will be amazed at the impact.

When one person sees a need and begins to address the need, soon you will see others begin to rally around to help in that endeavor.

During Your Journey... Be that ONE. Be the one who sees that the children need school supplies. Even if you can't help hundreds, you can help one. Be that one who sees the homeless person hungry. Even if you can't feed all the homeless, feed the one. It will make a difference. Just YOU be the ONE!

Follow God's Path For You

There are certain places that I like to go to on a regular basis; however, I do not travel the same route to get there every time. As a matter of fact, I know of many individuals who also head to that same destination, using a variety of routes.

It is important to note that while we all take a variety of routes to get "there," the destination is still the same. Furthermore, if I don't travel your way, it doesn't make it wrong - it just makes it different. If I ultimately get to that destination, what difference does it make if I don't take the same route as you? It may not be as quick or as efficient, but there may be something God has placed on my route for me.

Truthfully, there may be times when you even feel as though God's path is not the path that you want to take, but just trust me on this one. You will be much happier, and it will be just what you need - so much more than you could have ever wanted.

During Your Journey... Follow His path for your life. Don't allow the fact that you are not following someone else's path to success make you feel as though you are wrong. Just be sure that you are determined and focused enough to meet your goal. Also, don't hesitate to accept constructive criticism from those who have your best you at heart, and allow it to help you.

STARTING TODAY

The challenge with wanting to be better and do better is that we often don't know where or when to start. We often plan our path to greatness when the kids are older, or when we finish school, or when we get our promotion. However, this path doesn't have to wait. Start today. Allow everything that you are doing to better you and prepare you for your goal.

For example, if you are planning to be a newscaster, you will need to improve your public speaking skills, so record yourself while watching the news. If you are planning to do photography, begin taking pictures of even the smallest things - plants, trees, dirt roads - but begin today. If you are planning to become a public speaker, watch other speakers, learn what to do and what not to do. Not only watch them, but watch how engaged their audience is. Learn from it.

Ultimately, whatever you want to do, begin making preparations today to become it. That will minimize the amount of bad decisions you make because you will be constantly asking yourself, "How will this help me achieve _____?"

During Your Journey... Keep focused on your goals, and encourage yourself even when you feel discouraged.

How To Have A Productive Day

Every day is a gift. Let's maximize it to the fullest. Here's how:

- Get a good night's sleep, eat healthy meals, and exercise.

- Plan, document, and prioritize what you want to accomplish that day. Focus on high priority items.

- Strategize how you are going to manage your time to do so. Commit to your time budget for each item as much as possible.

- Keep the list visible and check off items as they are completed.

- Accomplish your tasks by alternating difficult and easy tasks. This will motivate you to continue and give you a bit of a break.

- Do a time remaining vs items completed check throughout the day.

- Reevaluate what is a priority and what can be moved to the next day.

- Celebrate success, and do it again tomorrow.

During Your Journey... Identify tools that will assist you in productivity. Just remember, sometimes that even means rest.

GREATNESS IS THERE

There's a TV show in which many individuals bid on abandoned storage lockers in hopes their bargain purchase will net a large profit as a result of its contents.

At first glance, the lockers usually appear disorganized and contents unusable. This is how the potential owners see the locker prior to the bidding process. However, after the storage lockers are acquired, the new owners begin to sift through the items, slowly looking for things of value.

The new owner will learn the locker's true value only if they first invest by purchasing it, then by analyzing it. , As a result of investing, people have come out with some great items, sometimes doubling or tripling the investment amount.

It's important that we do the exact same thing for ourselves. We need to invest in us, even when we appear disorganized and unusable, then search ourselves for the gems that are hidden deep below the surface's chaos. I am confident that upon that investment and research, you will find the greatness in you.

During Your Journey... Tap into the skills and talents that you possess, and begin the exploration process. You are bound to find your greatness. It's in there!

EXPAND YOUR CONNECTIONS

There may be aspirations in life on which we are struggling to get a handle. It might be different employment opportunities, more resources, or just more guidance, but we know we need more help. As we have done an assessment of our support system, we seem to be unable to locate the help that we need. Don't get discouraged! Do not be complacent, assuming that this is as good as it gets. I am convinced that the support is available, but we need to expand our connections.

Become proactive and seek out assistance. Get to know different people, and listen to their stories; you may find that your connections are closer than you realized. Also, share your story or vision with them, and hone in on any feedback they offer. Most people are truly willing to share their knowledge and experience. Let them!

During Your Journey... Connect to someone different today, and learn from them. As they empower you, they will also become more empowered. When your circle isn't large enough, open it up.

OBSTACLES = OPPORTUNITIES

We must take a moment to give more value and credit to perception. How we view obstacles and opportunities impacts our accomplishments. For example, if we view a new job performing new tasks as something we are not capable of doing, we then go into the position with "assumed" failure. However, if we go in with the "I can do anything" attitude, then accomplishment will be the end result. That is, of course, with proper training and support.

I used opportunities as the example here because if we are internalizing positive opportunities negatively, I can only imagine how we are perceiving obstacles. We have to see obstacles as opportunities. We then must take those opportunities and think positively about their benefits.

During Your Journey... Take that obstacle, allow it to be an opportunity, and then put your "I can do anything" attitude with it and watch yourself flourish.

Your Mind Determines The Matter

When my son was younger, he often challenged me regarding swallowing medication, he would declare that he couldn't do it. Well, on one particular day, I wanted him to try it again. Although he was not pleased with this, and stated that he was unable, I was not backing down and reinforced that he was.

So the battle began. After drinking a full glass of milk, he was still holding the capsule in his mouth. After a bit of yelling, gulping, and persistence, the pill was gone. He did it. Initially, he wasn't able to because he had already made up in his mind that he couldn't. As a result, there was nothing that could be done to change that. His mind had already determined the matter. Until he was shown otherwise.

Today, I would like to challenge you to do the same. Instead of making up your mind that you can't, decide that you can, then do it. Allow your mind to determine the matter.

During Your Journey... Make up your mind, and watch the matter become a reality. Just as I was the coach for my son in this situation, allow me to be your coach. You can do it. You can do it. Yes you can! Now let's get it done!

SEEING THE BEAUTY IN TURMOIL

One of my favorite types of art is abstract. It's the design in which you really can't see anything clearly but can see everything. One of my art pieces is by a very well-known artist who is extremely abstract in his creations. I remember a dear friend coming by and noticing the picture. She then commented that her young children could paint something better than what I had on the wall. In her mind, it was just chaos. However, I saw something different. I saw the beauty of what a variety of colors married together could create. To me, it was beautiful.

Now, I must admit, many of my friends and family felt this way about this work of art, but I stood my ground and proudly displayed it in my home.

Not everyone can see the beauty in chaos or turmoil. But if you can, then see it and stand proud. Accept that everyone isn't going to see what you see. Just because they can't see it doesn't mean it's not there.

During Your Journey... Look at the chaos in your life, look at the turmoil in your job, and recognize the struggles that appear to be spiraling out of control, but see the beauty and wholeness that you are going to become as a result.

Sometimes, You Must Walk Alone

There are so many instances when I wanted family, friends, or whomever to believe in my dreams and even help me execute them. Truthfully, most of the time, they did. However, there were some times in which they didn't. It wasn't because they didn't want to, but it was because they couldn't.

There are just some things that you have to go at alone. Friends and supporters are limited in what they can do in allowing your vision to manifest. So don't get discouraged because they won't go with you - they can't. Don't get angry when they don't execute the way you thought they should have. It's YOUR vision. You execute it.

There are some times when you must walk alone. The positive in walking alone is knowing that no other person can take the credit for what you have accomplished. Definitely acknowledge everyone as appropriate for their role, but it was you that brought it to completion.

During Your Journey... Don't be afraid to walk alone. And even if you are afraid, keep walking anyway. It helps to identify your hindrances because there's only you.

YOU WERE MEANT TO BE HERE

Recently, I was sharing with my daughter that I was very proud of her. She said thank you and then also said that she was fast. I wasn't sure what she meant by that, so I asked her to clarify. She went on to explain that she was fast because she ran the fastest to fertilize my egg. From that statement, I began to think about the reproductive process and how the sperm cells race to fertilize the egg. So she was right, she was fast.

Your presence is not an accident; it was by design. So embrace the fact that your very existence is intentional. Just as your birth was on purpose, your life has a purpose.

During Your Journey... Search for your purpose and perform it to the fullest. Live life to the fullest!

STRETCHING DURING DOWNTIME

There was a point in my life for about 8 months when I was unemployed. Because I had so much time on my hands, I began to do a bit of everything: coaching, counseling, training and development, and even a bit of website design. I used this time to do more than what I would generally do. I stepped out of my comfort zone and simply tried different things. This was an opportunity to tap into areas of me that I would not have otherwise utilized or had time to. I stretched during what I call downtime.

Your downtime may not be due to unemployment. You may be juggling a full-time job, a family, and school, but I still challenge you to do it. Stretch during your downtime. Take an hour out of your week to do something you have never done before. You may find that your passion has been dwelling dormant, waiting on you.

***During Your Journey*...** Challenge yourself to try something new. Step outside of your norm.

Your Vision Is Yours, Don't Give It Away

I attended a meeting that was full of those who are seeking to start or strengthen their businesses. What was interesting was that many people hesitated to share their business vision until the instructor reminded us that no one is inventing the wheel; we are all simply reinventing it.

While the attendees became more comfortable, vaguely sharing their pursuits, the instructor's statement really reinforced the hesitation for me. As people are seeking to make a living through their dream or vision, it's important that we don't give our vision away. But then I needed to really understand what giving my vision away really meant.

Giving your vision away isn't just telling someone about it, but it is also allowing others to do it, change it, or destroy it all together. So don't give it away. It might have to get delayed, but it can happen if you don't give up on it. So it's one thing to communicate about your business, it's something completely different to give someone else ownership of it.

During Your Journey... Keep your vision! Don't give it away! Keep working on it!

UNDERSTAND YOUR QUALITIES

Recently, I went through my emails and saw all of the positions that I had applied for at various companies. I received some callbacks, but for the majority, I did not. Either way, I am looking back at them and smiling because through all of the rejection, I had to take courage and stay encouraged.

I am grateful that I did not give up. I did not stop applying, and I did not change my goals. I stayed in the press and just kept saying, "Even if you don't consider me, I am still qualified."

We have to get to the point where we are confident in who we are and what we bring to the table. This may be a challenge for three types of people: 1) those who truly don't bring anything to the table, 2) those who allow others at the table to determine the worth of what is being brought and 3) those that don't know what they bring to the table.

During Your Journey... Take time to look at the great qualities of you. Look at the qualities on which you need to work. From that point, do your best to always allow your great qualities to shine, as you are improving on the others. It's okay to recognize your own qualities.

You Have To Want To

After a long day's work, I was really ready to head home. The traffic was heavy as usual, but it was uniquely heavy. There had been an accident on the expressway, and two lanes were blocked. For me, due to my desire to get home, it was a bit disappointing. While I was praying that the parties in the accident were okay, I certainly also whined a bit because I knew it would lengthen my ride home. And it did, but I got home anyway.

I had to take the long way home, and I endured heavy traffic all the way, but I made it home. My desire, drive, and will to get home is what got me there.

Regardless of the obstacles, roadblocks, and delays, I made it. Please know that you too can make it. Regardless of the obstacles, roadblocks, and delays, you can make it.

During Your Journey... Set your goals, and then make a plan B, just in case. And then go for it. You have to go on the journey to get to the destination.

THREE LESSONS TODAY

I remember a day when I left my check card with my husband in error. All week, I had brought lunch, except for that day, of course. I called my husband and reminded him that he had my card, and I had no money on me. He felt really bad and offered to drive about 30 minutes to bring lunch. I shared my story with my team, just smiling at the fact that he was so considerate.

Soon after, one of my co-workers quietly walked up to me, placed a $10.00 bill next to me, and told me to get some lunch. I initially declined because I figured I could stand to miss a meal anyway, but she insisted. Grateful just for the consideration, I accepted the offer and enjoyed my lunch.

Being down to literally change in my purse reminded me of how blessed I really am. There are some who don't have the support of a spouse, a peer, anyone, or anything to fall back on. When it's all gone, it's just gone.

During Your Journey... Remember these three lessons:

1. Be grateful for where you are… It certainly can be worse.
2. Treat people right… You never know from where your blessings will come.

3. As much as possible, save something, even if it's $2.00 a paycheck. There's nothing like being able to rely on yourself when you can't rely on others.

LEARN AND GROW ON

It is sometimes very difficult to locate your footing in life. You try several different avenues such as careers, spouses, and vehicles, and you still feel as if you haven't found a fit. What I have learned is that you choose your fit. This is identified by your reactions to various life situations. Regardless of the situation, you can determine your fit. Life doesn't happen to you but for you. Even the most negative of situations are a fit for you. They were tailor-made to strengthen and empower you, but it's up to you to decide. Choose to learn, live, and grow from every situation you encounter. Yes, some situations will be difficult, they will drain your strength and slow you down, but realizing that there is a growing opportunity will give you strength.

During Your Journey... Choose your fit, your placement, and embrace it. Life's lessons may get difficult, but they will be unforgettable. Learn and grow on.

Support Helps

Last evening, I did not make it to the gym, so I decided that I was going to work out a bit from home. There I was in my room with my son. I was on the floor, attempting to imitate the exercises that I observed on a video. As I began to exercise, I found that some of the moves were quite challenging and even downright difficult. So I began to just tell him how hard this was and that I was struggling.

Here he was, this skinny kid sitting in a chair, playing a game, and repeating everything that I had said to him. "Mom, don't you remember your empowerment moment? You have to exercise when you feel like it and when you don't."

"Mom, do you remember you said to me that if you think you can't do it, then you can't?"

So here I was, working even harder because he was giving me back the words that I teach and stand by (most of the time).

Finally, he looked at me then said, "Okay Mom, I am going to exercise with you." So he got down on the floor and proceeded to do what I had been struggling with on the video.

As a result of this experience, I learned two things: 1) support really does help, and 2) my son does listen to me.

During Your Journey... Find that person who is going to help you reach your goal. Allow him or her to speak difficult truths into your life and continue to work towards your goal. You can do it!

SOME THINGS MAY NOT BE IN BALANCE

We often hear about balance, but I am convinced that there is a time when balance isn't appropriate. I was thinking about my abundant love for others. I perceive and want the best for them and will assist anyone I can, but I then began to think about if and when they hurt me. Should I hate them as much as I have loved them? Should there be a balance in that scenario? Absolutely not! I can't balance love and hate, regardless of how thin the line is. I have to allow love to prevail and overcome hate, no matter how much I have been hurt.

Some things should not be in balance and truthfully will not be in balance. Such as love. It's okay to love unbalanced.

During Your Journey... Don't balance hate with hate, but overindulge with love, and it will eradicate the hate. Allow the love of God in you to supersede any anger, frustration, or un-forgiveness that you may feel. Love covers and heals.

Pour Out Of Yourself, It Wasn't About You

I celebrated the release of my first book, "Looking Back, then Moving Forward." I had such a great time with my dear friends and family who came out to support me. I was so grateful that they took time out of their schedule to come and fellowship with me in addition to purchasing a book. I wrote the book as a sort of release and freedom for me as I moved into my next stages in life. As I looked around the room, I saw those who had lost loved ones, those who had lost jobs, those who had their own successes that are worthy of celebration, those who were battling illnesses, those who had broken relationships, those who had troubled children or families - I saw people. Regardless of what their current challenges were, they put themselves on hold to support someone else.

They will never know how much it meant to me that they took themselves out of their normal routine to support me. One of the chapters in my book speaks about pouring into others and allowing them to pour into you. And this event was a reminder that it was never about me. It was a reason to celebrate but also a reason to focus on positive things that were happening instead of negative. This world is so much bigger than I am, and I would much rather have a positive impact than be a popular person.

During Your Journey... Give positive support and encouragement to others. Get yourself into a place where you can you can pour into others with no motives other than to give what God has placed in you to give.

THINGS TO REMEMBER FOR A GREAT LIFE

- Time Management - This is all that you get on this earth. Use it wisely. Once it's gone, you'll never get it back.

- Stay in Love - Fight for your love. Avoid the complacency of routines and find something every day to learn, absorb, and embrace about your love. Continue to cultivate it.

- Find Yourself - Love and accept the good and bad of you. Celebrate your quirks, as they are what make you different. If there is a need to improve, then do it. Love yourself enough to be better.

- Forgive - No matter what they did, why they did it, and who did it. Forgiveness is for you. It releases you from the bondage of anger, bitterness, and stress. Forgive and be free.

- Budget Well - My grandmother told me that it's better to have and not need than to need and not have. Don't spend every penny you get. Save some, spend some, and give some.

- Small Things Count - Look around and appreciate the small things in life. The trees, the rain, the colors of the seasons - they all are a part of God's

Creation, and if you pay close attention to them, they will remind you that life is truly a gift.

- Communicate - Don't be afraid to share. With clarity of thought, articulate your dreams, passions, and goals with confidence that you can achieve them. Being comfortable with who you are allows you to speak those things regardless of the obstacles and work to bring them to pass.

- Be an Example - Be an example to all that you encounter. Leave a legacy of greatness, pride, confidence, and love. One of the key reasons why parents are so special is because their role is to teach, protect, and provide. Leave your legacy as a teacher of knowledge, a protector of values, and a provider of wisdom.

BETTER OR WORSE

There is always someone in a better place than you and always someone in worse condition than you. That is what I was always told. But the question is, how do you handle either situation? How do you handle being around someone who is not in the same place as you? If you understand the context of both of these situations as well as how to handle them, you will be empowered as you interact with others.

There are times when you may feel as though you are not good enough to be with that person or group and other times when you are too good. Typically, the first thought is to disassociate yourself from them.

Truthfully, there are times when you should do that. However, the correct response is to understand their purpose for being in your life. Pay attention to the following things:

1) Are they becoming better as a result of your friendship, or are you becoming worse?

2) Are they draining you, or are you being strengthened by their presence?

3) Are you sharing in order to uplift them or is there little to no value in your conversations?

During Your Journey... Answer these questions during your interactions. You will know how to proceed regardless of the position that you are placed in.

What Label Matters

Can I just be a person? In these days and times, I am consistently slapped in the face with labels. Labels of social status, economic status, ethnic status, sexual orientation, job titles, personality types… just labels. But at what point can I be associated with being a person?

A mother, a wife, a sister, a friend, a mentor, a Christian, a person. If I must be defined, define me by something that is meaningful, something that will leave a legacy, a positive impact. My social, economic, ethnic, sexual orientation status – none of these things is meaningful when it's all said and done. But what is meaningful is if I have loved my brother and my sister.

If you must have a label, it should be created it by your character, your journey, and ultimately through the life that you live. Some of the labels with which I wouldn't mind being associated with are resilient, committed, determined, supportive…

During Your Journey… Think about how you want to be defined. What labels are important to you? What labels would you like to be associated with? Live your life in such a way that you will be.

Four Keys To Assessing Your Past

I have found that people spend a lot of time in their past. They are thinking and reviewing all of the that cannot be changed. However, I have also found that when they do they, it's a bit slanted only towards the negative events of life. So here are a few tips on how to correctly assess your past. NOTE: Use this assessment only as an instrument to move forward.

1. Review your total past. That means that as you assess what was done incorrectly, also assess what was done correctly. What were some things you did right? Where was your heart? What obstacles have you endured and overcome? Reflect back on your total past, not just your failures.

2. Identify the key lessons learned, think back to how you felt learning those lessons.

3. Forgive all parties involved in the situations that you are revisiting, including yourself.

4. Apply the learned lessons to your current state and your future. The mere application of the lessons learned is a key indicator that you are moving forward and are determined not to repeat them!

Pour Into Others Only What They Can Handle

Reality shows often depict big homes, fancy cars, and fine clothes and jewelry. However, we often forget to put in perspective that the reason why these rich and famous people are on television is because their lives are also filled with drama, dysfunction, and discourse.

Not that everyday lives aren't filled with chaos, but when we look at those who have what we desire to have, we must take a moment to look at ALL that they have. Once you take a look at the total picture, you will see that many of these celebrities are really in the same condition we are, except with more stuff. They are looking for lasting love, acceptance, and support. The problem lies in the fact that we look for these things in the wrong places. We look for depth in shallow areas, and it's just not there.

During Your Journey... Look beyond the surface of people, and if you see shallow, accept shallow, and invest only what they can hold. Conversely, if they are full of depth and complexity, then you will find that they may be able to contribute to you just as you contribute to them. This will help you to invest wisely, and the better investments, the better returns. Pouring a gallon into an 8 oz glass will only make a mess.

MIRROR THE GREATNESS

I can't imagine how many people work every day, attend school, and live what seem to be very normal lives but are depressed, sad, angry, disappointed, operating in an ocean of despair. It's especially difficult to see that in children. Recently, a young lady at the tender age of 15 shared with me that she had low self-esteem, had severe anxiety, and suffers from depression. While she had confidently accepted that diagnosis, she was still able to attain well over a 3.5 academically. My concern was that with all of the things from which I attempt to protect my children, there are that many more children who are exposed to life's tribulations without a support system.

If children are struggling, the most certainly adults are as well. But we can do something about it. We can encourage, support, and love them. We can help them see their greatness.

During Your Journey... Use the spirit of love to inspire hope in the life of others. Tell them they are beautiful and wonderful, without any expectation. Remind them that there are no limits if they keep pushing towards their goals. Assure them that things may be difficult, but they were hand-chosen to experience those things to help someone else. Tell them that they are purposed for greatness, but it's up to them to make it happen.

Once you pour that into them, look in the mirror and see the greatness in yourself. Acknowledge and celebrate the power that you have to change someone's life and ultimately the world for the better.

TEN KEYS TO GREAT RELATIONSHIPS

1. Be the kind of friend or colleague that you seek to have.
2. Choose those who will challenge you to think and to be better.
3. Choose those who are better than you in areas in which you seek to improve.
4. Embrace their teachings if they hold the values and integrity for which you stand.
5. Look for the greatness in people, not their flaws.
6. Don't pretend that flaws don't exist; true friends or colleagues will correct to build each other.
7. Strengthen each other during difficult times.
8. Choose those that have common core values and goals.
9. Communicate in the relationship, even during difficult times.
10. Focus on giving in the relationship.

GET UP

One morning around 6:00 am, I was up and moving around, getting ready for the day. I walked down the hall, and there was my teenage daughter, up, alert, and nearly fully dressed. I said good morning and then asked her why she was up so early. She looked puzzled at the question but then simply answered, I got up.

As I moved throughout my day, that three-word answer stuck with me: "I got up." I thought about the prodigal son, who came to himself, got up, and went back to his father›s home. I even thought about the resurrection of Christ, when He got up from the grave.

I thought about how the steps to greatness begin with getting up and not giving up. I thought about the journey of 1000 miles beginning with one step. Oh, how powerful.

During Your Journey... Get Up! Get up emotionally from the bondage of hurt, abandonment, neglect, and low self-esteem. Get up psychologically from the restraints of small thinking, insecurity, and self-doubt. Once we do, we will make significant strides in becoming better and our days will be more powerful and fulfilling.

GRATEFUL FOR RESOURCES

Going through my journey, I often come to forks in the road where I am not quite sure how to proceed. Truthfully, all decision points are not clear-cut, bad versus good decisions. Some decisions are which is better of the two good options or the best of the worst options that I may have.

When I am not sure which way to proceed, I turn to my resources. These are key people whom I respect, admire, and trust. I know that they have my best interest in mind and heart, whether I agree with what they are telling me or not.

During Your Journey... Talk to those important people in your life and tell them that you are grateful for them. They are a voice, a force, and a stabilizer in your life, and you appreciate them for that.

Do not hesitate to be that for someone else. The greatness, wisdom, and encouragement that you possess is in you to give to others. Go ahead and give it.

CAREER CHOICES

We often think that the job in which we can punch the clock, come in at 8:00, and leave at 4:30 is the job for us. It has little or no responsibility, it doesn't challenge us outside of our comfort zone, and when we are done for the day, we are done. Now, at first pass, that seems like the job to have, especially if there is a good salary and benefits involved. But let's take a closer look at that.

If you are late, you're penalized, if your kids are sick, you have to find a sitter, you have to be in a specific location to work, and if you miss a day, the excess work will be waiting for you on the next day – so now you are faced with double.

So what do you do? This quandary is very common for many, but not all, working people all over the world. For those very reasons, have you considered pushing for a career, not a job? A career that is mobile. A career that if you are late, it's okay because you probably already work from home at least a few times a week, and you're salaried, so your income isn't impacted. A career that if your kids are sick, you can call in to the meeting or simply work from home. A career that challenges you every day to be better, smarter, and a greater contribution to everything with which you interact.

During Your Journey... Think about your career choice and how it may or may not align with your life's desires. This may prompt you to set and reach different goals.

EIGHT STEPS татo A GREAT DAY!

1. Wake up and express gratefulness.
2. Plan your day with focus and purpose.
3. Eat healthy meals, and exercise.
4. Appreciate everything in which you take part, such as your cup of coffee or your drive to work.
5. Encounter every obstacle as an opportunity to become better.
6. Acknowledge each of your accomplished goals throughout the day.
7. At the end of the evening, celebrate your accomplishments for that day.
8. Look forward to completing even more tomorrow.
9. As you turn in for the evening, express gratefulness.

HOW TO REALIZE AND EXCEED YOUR GOALS

- Make your vision a priority - Even create visual reminders by posting it on your mirror, or send yourself daily or weekly reminders about your vision. This will keep you focused on your goal and minimize any tendency to push it down the priority list.

- Work towards your goals - Ensure that your activities drive you closer to your goal. For instance, if you desire to be a doctor, you should be pursuing medical school.

- Time - Remember that time is your friend - that is, if you use it wisely. Choose how you are spending your time and how much time you are spending pursuing your goals or doing other things. Commit to at least one hour a week working towards your goal.

- Celebrate small successes - Celebrate the small milestones that you make as you drive towards your goals. That way, you are able to measure your forward movement towards making your dreams a reality.

- Keep moving - Once your goal has been realized, begin to identify what is next for you and how you can accomplish it. We all have a purpose.

How To Find The Greatness In People

- Look for the greatness and expect greatness from them. Do not lower your expectations.

- Tell them you see their greatness. This will challenge them to seek and expose what you are able to already see.

- Communicate your expectations, and provide tangible feedback on how they can achieve it. Do this without being condescending.

- Acknowledge them when they have lived up to your expectations or at least are moving in the correct direction.

- Acknowledge their potential to be great, even when their actions haven't displayed it, disregarding the undesired behavior.

- Realize that you can't control others, but you can control you. So more than working on them, continue to work on you.

FIVE KEYS TO STAYING ENCOURAGED

Let's face it - in our careers, in our homes, in our schools, in our lives, times get hard. Things get difficult and sometimes downright discouraging. When those events occur, you begin to question yourself, your decisions, and your capabilities. But it is really in those times that you have to encourage yourself.

Here's how:

- Talk to yourself - Your mind will fill itself with self-doubt. When this begins to happen, instantly speak back, not out of emotions but out of facts. Tell yourself how wonderful you are and how smart you are. Remind yourself of your accomplishments that prove why.

- Stay close to people you know will support you and not judge you - Surround yourself with positive, uplifting people. Let them speak life into you.

- Post positive declarative statements in your area - On your mirror, put post-it notes there declaring your worth. Tape inspirational statements to your computer monitor.

- Know that there is a Higher Power, and He has ultimate control - If you have done all that you can do, rest in that.

- Engulf yourself in a positive environment - When you watch television, watch shows that are positive, funny, and encouraging. Even your music - if it's not positive and uplifting, don't listen to it.

LIVE ON PURPOSE

During the 2013 inauguration speech, every sentence that President Obama said was clear, concise, and purposeful. He was very aware of his limited time to deliver the speech, thus it had to be powerful, prompt, and impactful all at the very same time.

As individuals, we have to realize that life, just like the inauguration speech, has a definite beginning and ending. As a result, we need to ensure that every moment, every interaction, and every spoken word has purposeful meaning.

During Your Journey... Live life on purpose, use our words on purpose, and allow them to have lasting meaning.

Six Keys To Handling Challenging Situations

People encounter difficult situations every day. However, they often, are not equipped to handle them. The lack of skill along with the emotions that are connected to disagreements can make for a very bad situation. Here I have listed keys to handling challenging situations. These can be applied in every area of your life.

1. Address the problem, not the person. Remember that your ultimate goal typically is the same, but it's usually the approach that is the issue.

2. Gather all of the information. Ask questions that will help you make the best decision as possible. Listen to what is being said, rather than planning for a response.

3. Restate what you was heard, ask additional questions if needed.

4. List or discuss possible solutions based on the information provided and make the best decision.

5. Make the decision that will be best for all parties involved.

6. Look for the positives in the problem. Celebrate the resolution for three reasons: 1) you were able to come to a resolution, 2) it was a successful opportunity to increase your communication, listening, and problem resolutions skills, and 3) you were able to strengthen the relationship.

CULTIVATE YOU

Throughout this book, there is information primarily speaking about understanding yourself but pouring into others. During this new journey, I have found that in just a few short weeks, the workout that I initially struggled with is now too easy for me to do. As a result, I've had to increase the resistance on the equipment that I use, and I've had to increase the weights that I used for strength training.

The lesson is that if we are consistent, those areas in which we struggle will soon become easy to overcome. We have to keep challenging ourselves to become better, smarter, wiser, and in the case of exercise, healthier. Do something consistently that you know will benefit you. You'll be amazed at the results.

During Your Journey... Always work to improve you!

Two Times

What is that thing that you know you should do, but you just don't feel like it? Is it school, exercise, difficult conversations?

Whatever it is, I encourage you to do it. There are two times when you should do it: when you feel like it and when you don't. Some things just are not based on feelings. Using difficult conversations as an example, there are times when I do not feel like having the intense conversation about the sensitive topic, but because it is not about emotions, but the health of a relationship, I push myself even when I don't feel like it.

So what I have learned is this… There are two times when you should do something: 1) when you feel like it and 2) when you don't.

During Your Journey… There will be times when you don't feel like studying, exercising, having difficult conversations, but I encourage you to push past how you feel and do it anyway. You won't be sorry.

JUST GET THERE!

Today, I went to the gym - not really feeling like it, but I pushed my way there anyway. Walking into the door, there was a man that came in in a wheelchair. I greeted him and asked him how he was doing. He stopped and responded, "I am here." I then followed up with, "That's good; sometimes just getting here is half the battle.

During Your Journey... Things can seem so unachievable in life, but just the ability to get to the place where you can accomplish your goal is often half the battle. Just get there, and then you will accomplish your goal. So do it, get to the gym, get to work, get to school, get to church, and then you will be in position to win!

STAY CHALLENGED

You have to stay challenged in order to meet goals. While you may like where you are and what you are doing, it still may not be where you should be in order to accomplish your goals. What about you? Are you where you are supposed to be? If not, then move. You are only delaying or denying yourself if you don't.

During Your Journey... Allow the best in you to continue to flourish. As you do that, you will naturally see the expansion of who you are, what you contribute, and the difference that you can and will make in this world.

APPEARANCES

In the gym, it's interesting to see people with their hair matted and full of sweat as we strive to be healthier, stronger individuals. Looking at people at face value, one might assume that we don't have anything to offer. We may be perceived as unemployed, uninteresting, and unattractive.

However, that couldn't be the further from the truth. As a matter of fact, our physical appearance in the gym should be used as a metaphor for how hard we work or have worked in our lives to become and stay successful.

So don't judge appearances. Instead, identify and appreciate our passion, commitment, and work ethic.

During Your Journey... Look through the surface of those with whom you interact, and look into their hearts and minds. This is done by not only reviewing what is being said, but what is being done.

THE RESILIENCE IN WEEDS

Usually, when I am speaking about the lessons from exercise, I am sharing something that I learned from working out in a gym. The gym is my preference for strength training and exercise; however, over this past weekend, I learned from a completely different area. Nature…

I committed to my husband some time ago that I would do some yard work with him. To honor that, I was out in the yard pulling weeds, and they (yes, the weeds) taught me something… resilience.

As I was pulling the weeds, I noticed that there was a layer of dark fabric as well as newspaper on the planting beds. These items were supposed to keep the sunlight out and thus ensure that the weeds did not grow in those designated areas. However, they did. In spite of all of the preparation that my husband did to prevent the weeds from growing, they did anyway.

During Your Journey… Let's be resilient. In spite of all of the obstacles, challenges, darkness, and layers of problems that try to stop growth, if we are resilient, we can still grow. If we choose to grow, not only are we visible, but our strength and determination also will be recognized.

DETERMINATION CAN SPARK CREATIVITY

While on vacation, it was my best intention to go to the hotel's workout facility to exercise. However, I didn't. Instead, I walked up and down several blocks and quite possibly miles to enjoy the sights. So while not physically being at a gym, my goal to consistently exercise was still achieved.

As you are working to meet the goal that you have set, just remember there just might be several ways to accomplish that goal. Allow your determination to spark creativity when faced with challenging situations.

During Your Journey... Think about a goal you have set. Then think and maybe even document all the possible scenarios that you could utilize to accomplish it. You'll be glad that you did!

WORK AT IT!

Juggling multiple tasks can be a major challenge. Especially when you are constantly dealing with shifting priorities and overwhelming demand.

However, I have even learned something. It won't work if I don't work at it. I can't say that I am publishing a book if I don't write one. I suppose I can say it, but it would be just that, words.

My desires cannot be manifested if I don't do what it takes to accomplish them. In everything that I seek to achieve, I have to be diligent, consistent, and driven. Without these things, I am relying on chance. And while you may get a chance, being unprepared will squelch that quickly.

During Your Journey... Make your plans, then work your plans.

STAY CONNECTED

Using the treadmill has taught me a powerful lesson in connection. For anyone who has used a treadmill, you are familiar with the little string and clip that you affix to yourself to connect you to the machine. In case you slip or lose balance, this little mechanism is designed to disconnect you from the machine and immediately turn it off. It is designed for your safety, with the goal to prevent injury.

As long as you are connected, the machine operates at the incline and speed which you have designated. As long as you are connected, you are working towards your goal. As long as you are connected, you are active, and at your discretion, you can increase speed, incline, and overall challenge. But if you get disconnected, all of that stops.

During Your Journey... Stay connected. Stay connected to those people, entities, and resources that mean you good. Stay connected to those visions and dreams that are embedded inside of us. We have to stay connected to the support that will give us latitude to grow.

MOVE BEYOND YOUR EMOTIONS

Events and activities in life can all generate emotional reactions. Some reactions are positive, such as love and joy. Some are not such as anger and disgust. Emotional reactions are so powerful that they may cause you to behave in a manner different than you otherwise would. For example, one may not apply for a job because of fear or you may not ask for help because of distrust. As I began to think further, I realized that people make emotional decisions every day and these decisions our lives. It's not the emotions that change our lives, it's the behaviors that change them. So it's important to remember that our behaviors are the things that change our lives for better or worse, therefore it's imperative to keep our emotions in their rightful place.

During Your Journey... Move beyond emotions, and look at the goals. It's the behaviors that make the difference.

Never Too Late

One day at the gym, I took a moment to look around me. I slowed down just enough to see the diversity in those that were in attendance. I saw various ages, maybe as young as elementary school to the very wise and elderly age bracket. We were all in the same place doing the same thing, exercising. But what stood out is that we all have a goal. We gather in the same place, usually at the same time, to accomplish something, a goal.

What's interesting is that while we all had goals, I am sure they were all quite different. You may be seeking to rehabilitate from an injury, achieve a healthier lifestyle, or improve on sports abilities. Either way, we are working towards our goal.

During Your Journey... Please know that it's never too late to set a goal and work to achieve it. No matter what the goal is, as long as we are living, breathing, and believing, it's not too late.

OPPORTUNITIES

Throughout the gym are several televisions. On each of the televisions, there is typically a different show on, be it the news, a talk show, a home and garden show, and so on. While exercising, I glanced across all of the televisions, and it came to me. We have opportunities. There are so many variables that set one of us apart from the other, but that's what makes us unique. Never the less, we still are in a world full of opportunity.

During Your Journey... Recognize that there are opportunities all around us. We have to learn to take advantage of them. If it doesn't work in one place, surely it will work in another. That's where the persistence and diligence comes in. Look for your opportunities to shine, and take advantage of them.

Slow Down, But Don't Stop

Interval workouts on cardio machines are designed to push you to a very intense level of workout down to an extremely low level of intensity. This gives you somewhat of a break while it keeps you exercising.

Today, I paid quite a bit of attention to how I was managing my interval workout on the treadmill. Initially, my low level intervals were longer than my high intensity intervals. While that's fine, I realized it would take me longer to meet my goal using that method. Since I pride myself on not wasting too much time, I began to increase the time that I spent on high intensity intervals and decrease my low level intervals.

During Your Journey... The key to remember is to keep going. Whether it takes me longer than expected to achieve the goal, the only way that you can get to your goal is if you don't stop. It's not a time waster to pace yourself or move at a high intensity level, as long as you're moving. It's perfectly okay to slow down, but just don't stop pressing towards your goal. So slow down if you need to, but just don't stop!

TIME, RESOURCES, AND MONEY

In any project, there are three major things that can impact its success; resources, time, and money. Resources is the help or support that we may need to accomplish a task. While it may be discouraging to not have all of the support necessary, you now have this opportunity to leverage your creativity.

Time is often a challenge because we want to accomplish specific goals in a specific timeframe. Often when we don't, we just give up. And what that really means is that your goal will not ever be accomplished. You have to just remember the saying "It's better late than never". Let your accomplishment be late if it must, but let it be accomplished.

Money is the last major component needed for a project or, more importantly, for life. Often what we want to accomplish is challenged by the lack of financial means to accomplish them. However, I do believe that it is a test, in its own way of how badly we want it.

During Your Journey… There may be times when we may be short on time, resources, or money and it may force us to compromise. However, we have to always ensure that our compromise isn't at the expense of our integrity. Manage your life, using your time, resources, and money. But don't compromise you.

BE THE BEST YOU

In this world competition and drive, we often look at others in an attempt to take on characteristics that are found to be valuable. It could be a positive attitude, a great smile, or proactivity. There are so many characteristics that can be great for others to learn from and apply.

Our challenge is to look and learn from others without disregarding or devaluing who we are. The core of us, as God has made no other like us and if we spend our time trying to be what someone else wants us to be, then who will be us.

During Your Journey... Be the best that you can be. Allow what you learn from others to enhance you. Your goal is to because a better you, not an imitation of them.

Conclusion Of The Matter

Now that you have gotten to the conclusion of the matter, there are a several items things that I really hope that you have taken away from this book.

One being that motivation is truly all around you. It's just a matter of perspective. When you look at those that are doing well, choose to feel motivated to accomplish your goals just as they have accomplished theirs. When you see those that aren't doing so well, get motivated so that you can help them. Also, be willing to take on the responsibility to be a catalyst for change, and improvement.

The second item that I would like for you to take away is simply this… The only difference between the ordinary and the extra ordinary is the extra. What that means is when you do that extra. When you put that extra time in, extra effort, it will pay off. You have to believe that and operate as though it is so.

The third item is this, your dreams and visions need you. If you dream but don't pursue them, then it's nobody's fault but your own. You are responsible for what is in you. Others may influence you, but you are responsible and accountable.

The fourth item is this, begin to take a look at yourself as God sees you. Try to see yourself as God would see you. Think as he would of you, and then behave as though it's so.

Life's lessons happen on ordinary days but the applications of those lessons can lead to an extra ordinary life. He said that has thoughts of good and not evil towards you. Can you think of yourself in that same manner? I challenge you to do so.

So in conclusion, please realize that your daily living has generated extra ordinary lessons. Lessons that will make you better, smarter, wiser, more efficient, and more effective, if you allow them to. And nothing about that is ordinary!

MY FINAL THOUGHTS TO YOU!!

Just as you are finishing this book, I would like to end with this final thought and reminder. Everything that you need is in you. The innovation, the thought leadership, the passion, the intellect, the perseverance, the faith, the confidence, the hope, the drive… it's all in you. Thank you for allowing this book to share some insight that is really designed to just add a little bit of gasoline on your flame of success.

My prayer for you is that you take all that you have and use it to operate into your purpose. Thank you for taking the challenge and charge to move into it. I am confident that as you do that, you will be changing the world for the better, and I thank you in advance for that.

QUICK ORDER FORM

The Book of Extra List price $12.95

Website: www.celestecuffie.com

Email: lifeempowered@celestecuffie.com

For speaking engagements, or seminars, interviews, email, or mail request to the address listed above.

The Book of Extra

www.ingramcontent.com/pod-product-compliance
Lightning Source LLC
Chambersburg PA
CBHW071722040426
42446CB00011B/2180